Foreword by:
Lisa Lax and Nancy Stern Winters

On May 5th, 1977, in Ghana, West Africa, Emmanuel Ofosu Yeboah was born— and then abandoned.

Upon discovering Emmanuel had a severely deformed right leg, Dickson Kwadjo Ofosu, disgraced by his son's disability, walked out on his family. Emmanuel's mother, Comfort Yeboah, was advised to kill her son. But rather than surrender to society's perception that disabled children are the result of a family curse, Comfort neither killed Emmanuel, nor sent him to the streets to beg, as expected. Instead, she enrolled him in school and taught him to believe that he deserved the same treatment, opportunities, and privileges as able-bodied Ghanaians.

Today, against incalculable odds, Emmanuel is opening minds, hearts, and doors—and effecting social and political change throughout his country and in the United States. While Emmanuel's message—people with disabilities are valuable contributors to any society—is vital, his method is inspirational. Emmanuel began his quest with a bicycle ride, over 400 miles, across Ghana with one leg, and he continues to spread his vision with grit and resolve.

In 2005, Oprah Winfrey presented Emmanuel the prestigious Arthur Ashe Award for Courage at ESPN's ESPY Awards. The telecast was viewed by President Kufour of Ghana, who in turn stunningly invited Emmanuel to his Palace for a meeting. This was the first time in the country's history that a disabled person entered the presidential quarters. That day, President Kufour promised Emmanuel that he would bring the Disability Bill, which Emmanuel and fellow disabled citizens fought for, to the floor of Parliament. Six months later the bill was passed, changing and bettering the lives of millions. His unforgettable journey transcends continents and cultures.

We met Emmanuel a decade ago and knew immediately that he was a special young man with a giant vision. Three years later, we stood adoringly watching Emmanuel receive a standing ovation at a sold-out premiere of *Emmanuel's Gift* in New York City. He left the theater that night with tears in his eyes, and said "My mom would be so proud." As filmmakers, we feel extremely fortunate to have had the opportunity to tell his story in *Emmanuel's Gift*, and even more lucky to be able to call him our dear friend.

Written through the eyes of child author, Anthony Mazza, in collaboration with Emmanuel, we think you will truly enjoy reading this story, *A Mother's Love*, that illustrates Emmanuel's uniqueness, belief, love, respect, honor, strength, and vision.

We love you Emmanuel,
Lisa and Nancy

First Edition. Published in the United States of America.

ISBN 978-1-61660-008-2

Visit our web site at www.reflectionspublishing.com for more information or inquiries.

* * *

Other books by Reflections Publishing:

The Real Beauty: Navigating Through Divorce and Moving
ISBN: 978-1-61660-000-6
Written by: Kathryn Mohr
Illustrated by: Kiana Aryan

Remind Me Again: Navigating Through the Loss of a Loved One
HC: ISBN: 978-1-61660-001-3
P: ISBN: 978-1-61660-010-5
Written by: The Ster Family
Illustrated by: Colleen C. Ster

Face 2 Face: Navigating Through Cyberbullying, Peer Abuse, & Bullying
ISBN: 978-1-61660-002-0
Written by: Caroline Ster
Illustrated by: Emily Jones

Remember Me When: Navigating Through Alzheimer's Disease
ISBN: 978-1-61660-009-9
Written by: Isabelle Ster
Illustrated by: Emily Morgan

Scars: Navigating Through Peer Pressure & Consequences of Actions
ISBN: 978-1-61660-003-7
By Parent/Child Team:
Dave, Julian, and Noelle Franco

Crash: Overcoming Fear and Trauma
ISBN: 978-1-61660-006-8
Written by: Max Greenhalgh
Illustrated by: Jessa Weiner

Shining Through a Social Storm: Navigating Through Relational Aggression, Bullying, and Popularity
ISBN: 978-1-61660-004-4
Written by: Skylar Sorkin
Illustrated by: Sydney Green

Falling to Pieces: Navigating the Transition to Middle School and Merging Friends
ISBN: 978-1-61660-007-5
Written by: Sarina Rogers
Illustrated by: Mia Rogers

Tribute to Mothers:

To my mother, Paula, who is always there for me in my times of need
and there to help me pull through tough situations.
—Anthony Mazza

Mama Comfort, thank you so much for showing me that I have a gift,
and now that gift is a gift to many people in the world.
You are such a wonderful person. You came into my life and you are my hero,
and you are a hero to many women in this world. I know you are in heaven,
and you are still with me in spirit. I love you my darling Mother Comfort.
—Emmanuel Ofosu Yeboah

To my mother, Jean, and wife, Rosalind, for their love and support.
—Philip Trotter

To my mother, Rosemary, whose unconditional love and
strength-to-the-core continues to shape who I am today.
—Paula Mazza

There is no greater, more unconditional love than a love
shared between a mother and child. With heartfelt love to our mom, Ellen,
and our children, Sophie, Brian, and Danny.
—Lisa Lax and Nancy Stern Winters

To my mom, Rosalie, who overflowed with genuine love for everyone around her.
—Colleen Carter Ster

Special Thanks:

Many thanks to Challenged Athletes Foundation, Lisa Lax and Nancy Stern Winter,
and Oprah Winfrey for supplying many pictures for this book.

Charity:

A portion of sales from this book will be donated to EEFSA
(Emmanuel's Educational Foundation and Sports Academy).

Unique...

"Without my mom, I would not be here today.
My mom gave me the gift of life,
and just like you, I was born unique."

- Emmanuel Ofosu Yeboah

Right: Emmanuel's sister, Naomi; Mama Comfort; and Emmanuel at age 12.

Believe...

In Ghana, people who are born disabled like Emmanuel often become beggars because people don't believe in them and accept their disability.

"If you don't believe in yourself, others won't believe in you either. I believed in myself because my mother believed in me."

- Emmanuel Ofosu Yeboah

Right: A confident Emmanuel participating in the San Diego Triathlon Challenge in La Jolla, CA.

Love...

Whether you live with your birth or adopted mother, or a "mother figure," a mother is anyone who loves you and treats you like a mother should.

"Women like Mother Teresa and my friend Oprah Winfrey have been 'mother figures' to many children around the world."

- Emmanuel Ofosu Yeboah

Above: Oprah Winfrey presenting Emmanuel, and his good friend, Jim MacLaren, the prestigious Arthur Ashe Courage Award at ESPN's ESPY Awards Program.

Right: Oprah Winfrey with the first ever graduating class from the Oprah Winfrey Leadership Academy for Girls located in Henley on Klip, South Africa.

Respect...

When you give respect to others, you also encourage them to give respect to you.

"Children are our future leaders of the world. Respecting others, including your mom, helps you learn to be a good leader at a young age."

- Emmanuel Ofosu Yeboah

Right: Emmanuel providing inspiration to children at the Royal Seed Orphanage in Odipong Ofakour, Ghana.

Honor...

As we each weave our blanket of life,
our mother will always be in our hearts.
Our journeys and accomplishments will
be their greatest tribute.

"I believe my mother is still with me and is
trying to help me to honor her in my life."

— Emmanuel Ofosu Yeboah

Right: Authors Emmanuel Ofosu Yeboah and Anthony Mazza display a quilt created for
St. Emmanuel's Gift International School by the preschool and kindergarten children
that attended KidsGames at Solana Beach Presbyterian Church in Solana Beach, CA.

Strength...

One day, our parents will move on, and we will need to find our own way.

"My mom was my motivation and helped me to achieve my goals throughout my life. When she was gone, I was not sure how to move on and find my own way. I felt like I lost something big in my life, but I stayed strong and overcame my obstacles."

— Emmanuel Ofosu Yeboah

Right: Emmanuel proudly displays a bicycle originally donated to Willie Stewart, director of the possAbilities Program at Loma Linda University East Campus in Loma Linda, CA. Willie gave the bike to Emmanuel to ride in the Rudy Braveheart Triathlon Challenge.

Vision...

Keep your focus on what you want in life, set your mind to it, and work hard so you can make your dreams come true. You can even help make dreams come true for others!

"Mothers can truly create good people in this world through loving and believing in their children and teaching them to be unique, respectful, honorable, and strong."
— Emmanuel Ofosu Yeboah

Right: Emmanuel with Nana Professor Emeritus Daessebre Oti Boateng the Paramount King of New Juabeng Traditional Area (Koforidua) at the groundbreaking of St. Emmanuel's Gift International School. This school is located in the eastern region of Koforidua, Ghana.

4114U
(Information For You!)

Introduction written by:
Philip Trotter - Educator, Francis Parker High School

Each book in Reflections Publishing's "Kids Helping Kids Through Books" series comes with a support system of how to help families heal emotionally, socially, and spiritually through each difficult life challenge. *A Mother's Love*, written by Emmanuel Ofosu Yeboah and Anthony Mazza, touches on the difficult topic of being disabled, but demonstrates how determination and belief in oneself can overcome one's physical disabilities.

The history of the disabled has been one of struggle and accomplishment. In spite of long-standing prejudice and discrimination, there are countless examples of individuals who have overcome seemingly insurmountable obstacles to achieve great things. In the early 20th century, Helen Keller overcame the limitations of her multiple disabilities to become a tireless activist and one of the great social reformers in American history. The 20th century also gave us President Franklin Roosevelt, who led the United States through the Great Depression and World War II, despite being crippled by polio. Both of these famous individuals had the unflagging support and encouragement of those closest to them. Helen Keller had Anne Sullivan, her teacher and mentor for nearly 50 years. President Roosevelt had his wife Eleanor, who supported and advocated for him throughout the darkest days of his presidency and is considered by many to be one of the greatest first ladies in American history.

Today, those with disabilities, especially in the developing world, continue to face an uphill battle for the rights and respect most of us take for granted. Emmanuel provides a model for those with disabilities all over the world who may feel the sting of prejudice and discrimination or the isolation that can come without the support of friends and loved ones. Of course, for Emmanuel, his greatest supporter and inspiration came from his mother, a woman who would not allow her son's aspirations and drive to be limited by his disability. Like Helen Keller and Franklin Roosevelt, Emmanuel once again reminds us that our potential and accomplishments can transcend the physical limitations of the bodies we inhabit, and that social and political barriers can be shattered by those who have love and support in their lives.

Franklin Roosevelt was able to calm a nation gripped with fear, Helen Keller dedicated her life to issues of social justice so everyone might enjoy the same rights and opportunities, and Emmanuel provides a simple model that if you believe it, you can achieve it. One of the many lessons we can learn from these amazing individuals is that we all have the ability to affect social and political change, that a message of hope and justice cannot be constrained by physical limitations, and that inspiration can come from anyone, anytime and anyplace around the globe.

Emmanuel sees the world as it should be, and has used the lessons taught to him by his mother and his own boundless energy and drive to provide inspiration, hope, and courage for those who are fortunate enough to know his incredible and moving story.

Action Steps to Help Families Emotionally

Written by: Challenged Athletes Foundation

The Challenged Athletes Foundation (CAF) is a unique nonprofit organization that recognizes courage, rewards perseverance, and realizes dreams. It helps people with physical challenges live full, active lives through participation in fitness activities and competitive sports. CAF believes that involvement in sports at any level increases self-esteem, encourages independence, and enhances quality of life. The ability to lead an active lifestyle is essential to emotional health, and CAF is dedicated to helping physically disabled individuals achieve active lifestyles and live life free of limitations.

Over the past 18 years, the Challenged Athletes Foundation has raised an excess of $36 million and satisfied more than 6,100 funding requests from physically challenged athletes nationally and internationally. Through CAF's Access for Athletes program, more than $1.7 million has been granted to physically disabled individuals in 27 countries this year alone. The cost of adaptive equipment such as running prosthetics, racing chairs, and handcycles, along with coaching and travel expenses, is often what keeps physically disabled individuals from leading active lives.

Together, the Challenged Athletes Foundation and the athletes it supports help to inspire others to reach for their dreams and achieve emotional health. Many CAF-supported athletes become mentors and trailblazers who help the next generation of physically challenged individuals find hope and success in sports. CAF and its athletes change perceptions among able-bodied populations and constantly redefine "what is possible." These athletes are the purest demonstration of the famous Bill Bowerman quote: "If you have a body, you're an athlete." Any obstacle can be overcome with a little encouragement and unwavering support, and when individuals begin overcoming obstacles, they begin to heal emotionally and flourish in life.

Action Steps to Help Families Socially

Written by: Philip Trotter - Educator, Francis Parker High School

Emmanuel's Model of Belief
Dream, Believe, and Achieve - Emmanuel Ofosu Yeboah

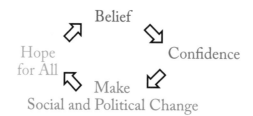

⇨ Your belief in yourself gives you confidence
⇨ Your confidence empowers you to make social and political changes
⇨ Your achievement in making social and political changes gives hope to all people

Belief

A belief in your own abilities is essential in all that we do. Success in school, sports, work and our personal life is tied directly to a belief that we can be a valuable contributor to the well being of others. Emmanuel was instilled with the belief of his own abilities through the mentors in his life and from his mother. He has chosen to empower others so that they too can lead.

Confidence

Confidence, Commitment, and Concentration provide the formula for most successful athletes and activists. Success in leadership comes from the belief that our contribution to a goal or cause can make a difference. Emmanuel provides a voice for thousands of people who live on the margins of society. His confidence in himself and his cause empowers others to seek change.

Make Social and Political Change

With privilege comes the responsibility to help those who are less fortunate. Success in helping those that struggle also brings meaning to one's own life. We should look at activism as an opportunity to lead a more fulfilling life. Although he has achieved more accolades in his life than most people, Emmanuel is not self-absorbed. He has chosen a life of service to others because of the need he feels to pass on his wisdom and energy to those who still suffer.

Hope for All

Each day brings the promise of new beginnings. We can be powerful agents of change if we choose to live our life for others. Success comes from our effort to touch others lives in a way that they can become empowered and hopeful. Emmanuel provides a symbol of what we can achieve if we put our mind and spirit to action.

Action Steps to Help Families Spiritually

Written by: Paula Mazza, Director of Preteen Ministries, Solana Beach Presbyterian Church

Celebrate Uniqueness

It's true. Never, in the history of mankind, have two people been created identical. Every single time a baby is born, something entirely new enters the world. Even identical twins are not 100 percent identical—just ask them. The Bible tells us that while we are all created unique, we are also created in the image of God. I like to think of this image as an enormous mosaic. Each one of us has the ability to reflect God's image in a way that only we can, simply due to our own unique design and internal wiring. In other words, each one of us is a tiny tile within this large mosaic reflection of God. If one of the tiles is missing, then we cannot see the complete beauty of the picture. Every time we choose to see someone through this lens, there is an opportunity to expand our understanding of who God is and what He is like. When we choose to overlook or bypass someone, we miss out on that opportunity.

Emmanuel's mother chose to CELEBRATE his UNIQUENESS, even though he was born into a culture that screamed otherwise. God is also all about restoration: bringing light into darkness, rebuilding what is broken, taking something old and making it new again. Ghana is a nation that was plagued with stigmas, superstitions, and misgivings centered around certain types of physical uniqueness. Then came Emmanuel and his story. Like you and I, Emmanuel wears his uniqueness on both the outside and the inside. But this story of redemption didn't actually start with Emmanuel. It started with a mother who looked at her baby boy, saw his unique physical shape, and knowing the likely reality that he would live life as an outcast, made a choice to reject that reality and speak a new truth into him. God worked through Emmanuel's mother to make a new reality—not just for Emmanuel, but for an entire nation.

Every day, you have an opportunity to follow the lead of Emmanuel's mother and be a part of God's continuing story of restoration. Here are some ideas for you and your family:

- When meeting someone new, ask yourself, "How is this person unlike anyone I have ever met?" As you get to know them, ask, "How does this person's uniqueness reflect God in a way that only they can?" and "How can I help this person celebrate their uniqueness rather than second guess it?"
- As a family, spend time discussing and celebrating ways that each family member is unique (i.e., "I just love that freckle on your nose" or "I really like the way you laugh" or "I think it's cool the way you…").
- Find something to "restore" as a family project. For example, go to a garage sale or thrift store and find something very old or broken that you can work on and give a new life. A fresh coat of paint does wonders to an old picture frame! Take it one step further by then donating your creation to a charitable organization and then have a family discussion on the concept of restoration.
- Find a way to serve others in your community. It could be as simple as spending a designated time picking up trash in a public area, or you could volunteer time helping at one of the nonprofit, community-oriented organizations in your area.
- Spend time reflecting on what the following verses mean to you and your family:
  - **Psalm 139:14** I praise you because I am fearfully and wonderfully made; your works are wonderful, I know that full well.
  - **Genesis 1:27** So God created human beings in His own image, in the image of God He created them; male and female He created them.